Drownproof

Drownproof

Peter Vanderberg

Black Centipede Press

Black Centipede Press
Denver, CO
blackcentipedepress@gmail.com

ISBN: 978-1-7353275-2-5
Cover Art: James Vanderberg, *Pulled in Pushed out*
Layout and Design: Brian Clint

For Sara, Thomas, Lucas, & Dylan,
may you be forever drownproof

Contents

Through the sea was your way;
your path, through mighty waters,
though your footsteps were unseen.

— Psalm 77

Seascapes

HMS Woolwich
13 January, 1806

Commander Beaufort begins his journal,

Hereafter I shall estimate the force of wind according to the following scale

0. calm
1. light air
2. light breeze
3. gentle breeze
4. moderate breeze
5. fresh breeze
6. strong breeze
7. near gale
8. gale
9. strong gale
10. storm
11. violent storm
12. hurricane

*

Beaufort gauged what each wind would allow:

light air.

bare steerageway with all sails set clean & full

Lookouts watch seascapes —

from lifelines

to horizon

watch —

small wavelets *glassy crests unbroken*

watch —

scattered *white* *horses*

name this wind *gentle breeze*

another *gale*

*

Sailors know when *sea heaps up*

& *white foam* *streaks off breakers*

at home *whole trees are moving* —

if she is out walking

her hair blows wild

& the wind resists her leaving.

*

Naming the invisible by how it moves

the visible

knowing seen & unseen —

the lookout feels breeze-borne
gale

forecasts *storm*

& another ship
will return from sea.

Light Breeze

glassy crests unbroken
wind felt on face

weather vanes turn

it was a perfect day
it was
the last perfect day

First Night at War

Underestimating your enemy
means thinking he is evil.
Thus you destroy your three treasures
& become an enemy yourself.
— Lao-tzu

Off the coast of war General Quarters woke the hive.
Helmets & flack jackets donned on the run toward deck
guns. I heave open a watertight door: Horizon flash —
no thunder. Another. Between mute bursts I face
Afghanistan & remember the Pashtun. Unwritten
nomadic laws demand revenge & asylum.

My ghost sits with tribal elders drinking chai,
translating the word *enemy.*

Or I am the enemy sending bullets to hearts & minds.

Or I am safe at sea squaring my fear of death
with those deaths silently brightening my horizon.

Near Gale

Between imagination & truth   memory grew fingers

        in my mother's womb as she wrote
her thesis paper: "Ripples of Surrender —

Japanese Literature After World War II."

                          Every cup of tea poured ceremony.

Mother-writer   thinking over horizons
        of psyche   took sides with a people
her father was sent to kill.

She shared   their death-resistance
against the conquest   of American men.

Her first child was birthed under threat of the knife.

Asian Studies called   from high bookshelves
                over games of war & backyard adventure.

Tall enough to reach   I found Bushido
                        & mountains
of recluse poems scratched   on trees & temple walls.

            Strange prophesy — water-bound son,
reading haiku   off the coast of Pakistan

standing watch so his ship doesn't   drag anchor

or loosen the grip of deterrence.

I am the gray warship
between their children & the winded sea.

I am insignificant.

I am writing to apologize.

Gentle Breeze

scattered white horses

leaves & small branches
in motion

I taught my children
a game called *war*

Water-born

He hushed the storm to a gentle breeze,
and the billows of the sea were stilled.
— Psalm 107

1

Beloved,

For your first days we began saving daylight —

lengthening hours

drawing thinner shadows.

On your first mornings: starlings crows
you have always been with us.

After a sleepless night we stood
the morning watch together.

Gull calls reminded me
there was a sea of days before you.

Now you sleep so still
I look for reasons to fear —
look for reasons not to

in your blind water-born eyes.

2

Our paces measured sea & cloud-locked sky
gulls warned us   gliding against wind.

Waiting   lungs too full to breathe counting
tiles   I watched doors
from the corners of my eyes.

Ranges of wife & daughter hearts
opening negotiations across the EKG:

my presence   was your mother's grip
when the strain broke vessels in her eyes.

Deep blue & frowning like a Hindu god
you woke crying for us all   pausing
for my impossible promises.

You were born in a panic of love & instinct,
as were your mother   & grandmothers before.

3

One night at sea   you were born in a dream.
Crying on a table
        I was the only one   who would bathe you.

        Years later   prayers weren't enough.

Your mother called on an older god.

Another dream:

first time I held you waking dream my funeral
you — archangel I — sinner at the gates.

You did not judge *there is only revelation.*

We will be revealed through our gaits
our solitary habits the ways we seek

& resist our sources.

I promise to give you all my weakness. You'll learn

your strengths when I am not teaching.

4

You are healthy,
growing faster than we thought,

you always will be.
Bones

flash in ultrasound
bright silver & fleeting.

You moved. *A boy.*
Your mouth was open (a boy).

arc of scull   ribcage spine

Your name means *tide flow*   means
born near the sea   *son of waves.*

Be born soon.

The wars are not going well

& people everywhere begin to despair.

Sea Heaps Up

Sara wants me to read her book. I want to watch the news. We try both. Between pages of Little Bear & Mama Bear making cakes, the story of a soldier home from war. After nights & days of screaming his daughter would pull away & say, *You're not my daddy.* He saw the dead in waking dreams walking with his daughter lying on the couch, wordless mouths opening & closing.

Sara presses her hand to my head & pushes back to the page saying, *read daddy, read book.*

"So Little Bear went all by himself — all by himself in new snow."

He went for help at the VA hospital but deployment rumors leaked & he locked himself in a room with Death.

After the news Sara molds my face like play-doh until she forms one she knows.

Man Overboard!

No one noticed the sailor swallow horizon before he jumped. No one heard his laments over seahawk rotors & engine roar. He leapt like a cigarette butt flicked into wind. From the flight deck ocean snaps bone, erases mind — but it will hold you up to say good-bye to air & sun. What longing for home? What solitude on a ship of three-thousand souls sent him over the side?

The penalty for despair is Captain's Mast — *Endangering lives other than your own.* Master-at Arms will take him to a seahawk, bound for the brig back home.

Home   is the new   exile.

Violent Storm

foam patches
cover the sea

visibility
almost lost

kyrie eleison

First Dogwatch

After the intel brief I step through a hatch & pray as red cloud-waves ignite the sea violet.

Dhow Close Astern

Through the Straits of Hormuz dhow boats swarm. Fishermen & merchant smugglers worked these waters for thousands of years before we stood watch on warships — arms crossed, scowling down at the traffic of dhows. Any wooden boat painted bright yellow & green, crewed by sons, could be full of a death triggered by prayers.

We enter Arabian waters as if we own them. As if the dhow captains read our Notice to Mariners: *Stay clear 500 yards,* or risk force from pencil flare to live fire in a last heartbeat.

Every boat crosses our bow too close. Lookouts warn: *Dhow, close astern!* Our sentinels grip deck guns wired tight to rip tracer rounds through any (credible) threat. I suspect every dhow captain wants us dead. I suspect every one of my gunners wants to sink a dhow.

Mass Casualty Drill

Bodies lined on the flight deck warm in the sun, joke & fake death. Clear skies, light breeze: perfect day for a Mass Casualty Drill. Doc leads his new guy over to practice CPR.

The dead man shouts, *He's not gonna kiss me is he?*

On the bridge they wear helmets & hesitate over laminated procedures. Fill berthing spaces with black smoke, sea water, limbless mannequins. It's my turn to reach for the captain with a fake wound in my face & mouth the words, *Help, it's not bad but I need to go home.*

He'll pretend to pretend I'm o.k. as I'm carried to the flight deck & lain beside a dead sailor tangled in nightmare: *this is not a drill.*

Drownproof

[lauds]

Stay optimistic. Our time adrift is likely to be brief & relatively comfortable. Tell motivational stories: There once was a fisherman lost at sea. He collected rain water, ate fish. Four months later he walked ashore, drownproof.

[prime]

The life raft is equipped with everything we need: first-aid kit, compass, pocket knife, signal mirror, blankets. Learn survival before disaster. Train for the unimaginable.

[terce]

Without water, delirium comes within four days, death in ten. Drink rain. Do not drink urine. Do not drink seawater.

[sext]

Tear cloth & weave into fishing line. A hook can be made from a safety pin. Ocean fish can be eaten raw. However, avoid poisonous:

trunkfish

pufferfish

toadfish

stonefish

parrotfish

triggerfish

cowfish

boxfish

filefish

lumpfish.

Sea birds may land on our raft. Kill & eat immediately. Feathers can be used to insulate clothing, bones make fish hooks, beaks make lures. The downy breast can be made into a hat.

[nones]

Don't trail hands or feet in water if sharks are present. If we can kill a shark, they are good to eat. However, the blood of a shark will attract other sharks. Screaming underwater may put off an approaching shark.

[vespers]

After a time adrift at sea, one may stand still & weep. One may dive off the raft to "go below for a cup of coffee." Make short term personal goals. Maintain faith in America by singing patriotic songs.

[compline]

Never press spiritual considerations if doing so divides the group or creates dissension. Exercise personal religious rituals, if any. Practice silent meditation.

[matins]

If no life raft is available, "play dead" to stay alive at sea. Face down, arms & legs loose — relax. Lift your head to breathe & scan horizon for birds, boats, flotsam. Do not waste energy screaming (unless sharks are present). In this way you can drift for days — drownproof.

Lost at sea

bridge-wing lookout —

calculating what time it is
back home
what season of trees.

I stare down to the bow wake   frothing

phosphorescent algae
& remember

sitting in church   lost

in the homily

staring at electric prayer candles

tiered below St. Anthony's feet.

Both lights reveal the dark

god

in whom I drown.

Celestial Navigation

for Liz

The ship's deck slowly rises & settles
on the night sea. I study celestial charts,
track a satellite's red-pulse through binoculars.
As the moon ripens over the black horizon
I bend memories with Mercator lines past home
& all the girls who lingered far enough away,
orbiting at a safe distance.
The woman in the moon is full now,

mouth slightly opened in a half-smile, half-
gasp surprise. She blushes with another sunset.
I settle between swells on the memory
of her who eclipses ship, sea, stars —
          Whispering into the ocean's ear
          I wait for her salty-sweet breath.

Gale

crests break into spindrift

twigs break off trees
walking made difficult

the wind warns
return *return*

Reading Leaves

Chance is buried under hope & weather.
Storm pushes one ship home — calls another away.

On Seaview Avenue they call Mrs. Shandel
when the moon promises birth, marriage or death.

A mother arrives at my door, asks me her life.
She wants me to read for her Johnny overseas.
What would you have me tell her?

Tea swallowed, the seer instructs:
swirl the leaves & turn the cup over.

Fortunes cling to the rim.
Her face clings to her child.

Our men don't return anymore.

Wind shift, storm clouds — the leaves
promised we would come home.

Water-worn

She was rollin' like crazy, seemed I could touch the waves.
Lost two aircraft & the false-bow — tore right off.

Over coffee at the kitchen table my grandfather
tells sea stories. He is water-worn.

Had to be towed into port — humiliatin'!
I missed all the action after that:
Guam, Wake Island, never saw any
action other than that storm.

Outside there is no wind.
Clouds have forgotten to be troubled.

The ship sent to replace us got hit by kamikaze
right on my gun-mount. The same one
I woulda' been at — totally destroyed it.
I felt bad fa' dose guys. That was a hellova' storm.

Grandfather Myths

I ever tell you 'bout the time I saved the ship?
A sneaky sub shot a torpedo in our side so I jumped
in the water & plugged the hole with my finger.
That's how come my finger is crookit'.

But that wasn't all, enemy planes were comin'
so I jumped in a hellcat to fight 'em off.
I was doin' great too until one of the lousy bastids
shot my wing — had to bail out over a jungle island.

Well that wasn't so easy either cause I landed
in a giant spider's web. Lucky I had my knife wit' me
so I could cut loose, but the spider came at me
wit' boxin' gloves on all his feet.

He didn't know I was the PS 212 boxin' champ though.
Pow! Knocked him right off his own web.
Sure! The navy was fun. They wanted me to stay
but ya grandma made me come home.

Scattered White Horses

What is strange is not the stories my grandfather told
or that I believed I too could be a man.
His finger *was* bent at forty-five degrees & I had recently
been given my first pocket knife: proof of mythology.

What is strange is not that I grew up on the brushed-up
waters of the Great South Bay under the out-to-sea
gaze of a father who was his best at the ocean gathering
driftwood furnishings, sending his sons back to shore.

What is strange is not that I joined the navy out of fear
of becoming an ordinary man, as if making decisions
out of fear isn't ordinary. As if choosing myth
over the daily compositions of life isn't ordinary.

Strange that mythology requires such few proofs:
seagulls crying over my father's house,
my grandfather's bent finger, knife in my pocket —
& that these made other worlds less strange to me.

Strong Breeze

whistling in wires

open umbrellas
become difficult to handle

letters from home
become difficult to handle

Mail Call

Dear P,

We're close to radio & T.V.
waiting for news all day.
Wondering what we are headed for.

Wish they wouldn't give away so much.

[Divine services are now being held in the library.
Maintain silence about the decks,
knock off all games of chance.]

I pray every time I pass St. Jude in the kitchen.

*

O St. Jude,
patron saint of hopeless cases.
Please watch over
our beloved.

Amen.

The Watch Officer's Guide to TAO

I drift like a wave on the ocean,
I blow as aimless as the wind.
— Lao Tzu

Nowhere is there a parallel

in the hands of

every moment

TAO
is especially important because
the watch
belongs to

TAO

Open yourself to the TAO,
then trust your natural responses
& everything will fall into place.

*

the officer at sea

is required to keep

TAO

to make sure that he understands clearly

If there will be fog
If he is wise

Can you step back from your own mind
and thus understand all things?

*

vision, both outside & inside
must extend beyond

his watch

a sense of proportion
when
every instant
darkened

the calm of a Sunday afternoon at anchor

Darkness within darkness.
The gateway to all understanding.

*

time at sea

will awaken

special talents

things begin to sort themselves out

Prevent trouble before it arises.
Put things in order before they exist.

*

human understanding
might not be readily available when wanted.

the essential

TAO

should be studied carefully

As an old salt said: "Relieve in haste, repent at leisure."

Rushing into action, you fail.
Trying to grasp things, you lose them.

*

Things to be avoided:

1. clumsy or redundant language

2. emergencies
3. word that is not of concern
4. church except in emergencies
5. a long list
6. use of the phrase “now bear a hand”
7. demands
8. Pauses, hesitations, & breaks written down

on watch

there are many occasions

when a touch of humor is

disaster

coax your mind from its wandering
& keep to the original oneness

*

Erasures

bring validity

into question

The Master observes the world
but trusts inner vision.

*

All vision depends on
a slow roving gaze

Do you have the patience to wait
till your mud settles & the water is clear?

It is the proper way to begin.

Forenoon Watch

Engine Room rounds — I find Machinist Mate Bruce
wavering behind the boiler, staring down a gauge.
His eyes, dull like a sick animal's, are slow
to distinguish me from machinery or memory.
I ask how his big date was.

Sir, (he laughs) she tasted like peach cobbler.

Not peaches, but cobbler: that home sweetness,
ripe fruit, softened, wet, broken crust.

Bruce leads me to the devil's chair.
Between bulkhead & furnace, one needle trembles
just below catastrophe. Iron heat evaporates thought.

Look sir, my damn kneecaps sweat through my pants.

The pitch of Bruce's laughter rises to fever,
then drowns in the groan of turbines.

Evening Watch

The ocean begins to look like home

sound like a voice

calling through nightmare

calling me to wake —

Wake fires & a distant ship

steady my gaze

on a line

where pitch meets night.

[Taps, taps, lights out,
all hands turn into your bunks.]

Make course for true wind.
Drive bow through swells

[Maintain silence about the decks.]

so the crew sleeps through the night.

Chief Fisher's Song

Forty-sixth day at sea: the crew has earned a Beer Day.
Chief Fisher whispers to the horizon,

Beer said the blind man!

He never explains. He wants his ration cold.
Beer Days on *his* first ship resounded in throats full of,

Beer! said the blind man!

Each can opened ports in Japan, Thailand, Australia, oh!
Australia, where girls waited for ships at the pier

& we never paid for beer, man!

Two cans of beer turn flight deck into steel beach
as sailors go blind to all before Beer Day singing:

Beer! said the blind man!

Back on the bridge, the froth of Beer Day sours
as the watch cycles back to paranoia.

Strong Gale

sea begins to roll
foam blown in streaks

slates torn from roofs

we begin to translate lines
drawn across the sea

Walk on Water

Tuesday of the 18th Week
in Ordinary Time

The following message
came from the Lord:

your wound is cause
for your healing

your lovers have forgotten
your sins

take the deadly risk
of approaching me

I will build
this written heaven

watch the sea

it is a ghost

walk on water

toward God.

Hurricane

sea completely white
with driving spray

countryside devastated

trees uproot
our prayers

Psalm for the Last Day of Summer

Among mussel encrusted breakers
revealed by dead-low tide,
plovers scavenge the day's sacrifice.

In the shallows between beach & sea,
my children tumble in the surf, surprised
by sand giving way beneath their feet.

We come at this late hour to face ocean
& burn once more, speaking scattered tongues
which even our beloved misunderstand.

It was a good day. Tomorrow we may
incite another war. We may need to draw
upon the slow burn & plover's call

when the tide brings our children (God
forbid) something other than laughter.

Spindrift

Teaching U. S. History, I mark timelines with wars,
fill in the blanks with questions:

What are the causes?
What cost? What effects?

Hall duty premonition: student ID faces
reminded me of News Hour *Honor Roll* faces.

The anchor offers, *here, in silence, are ten more.*
None smile. Uniforms sharp as broken glass.

I try to learn their ages & hometowns
before they fade & the next appears younger,

or older, from another place where the cost
of war is history & each day less believable.

Jamall Jacobs, grade 11,
don't join the marines.

*

I see you shot in a street
by someone you never see.

You'll run down lists of everything
you didn't forget:

body armor   *stay low*
head on a swivel

Searching for the cause of your pain disbelief will fade
back to boot camp — to Maria from 2nd Division —

to Long Island City —
to your mother

who eases you down the wall
& rests your head on gravel singing,

everything's gonna be alright,
everything's gonna be alright now.

The Counting

In the news today — as most days —
car bomb kills twelve. Another kills eight,
kills forty-one. My son has just begun
to learn numbers. He tells me,
the counting never stops:
his first lesson in the infinite.

One, killed in the market bombing,
was five years old, out shopping with his mother.
She examines melons, counts each coin,
wants ripe fruit for her son who asks questions
about the man selling melons.
She shushes him, chooses & pays.

Nearby, a local martyr can be heard
praising God, certain of His will.

Calm

sea like a mirror

— no wind —

mirror like a sea

Mirror Sea

What we must take as the object of our attention
is not the dream as a whole
but the separate portions of its content.
— Sigmund Freud

1

Trapped

below deck
between steam pipes

through air ducts & vents

until tight spaces

grew hot from the boilers

& I knew

no escape.

*

At sea I dreamed of life back home.
Home, I dream of being called back
to sea, to war & all these lives

are the dreams I must forget

before they turn from nightmare
to the siren songs I'll sing to my children.

2

Sea & Anchor Watch —
                                        no one knows
how to navigate.

Newly called back
                    I keep quiet.

The ship leaves
harbor at full speed   dragging anchor
        ramping over the outer jetty to sea.

*

Every cigar on the smoke-deck
celebrated another day
we fooled each other.
Not good to be alone too much.

When I start speaking to the sea
I've been alone too much.

3

Letter from   Department of Defense
    War: called back:
due at my ship yesterday — no good-byes.

In the ship's store I purchase:
                envelopes
                pens
                vienna sausages
                brass Zippo

*

Joining the military
provided excuses:
the myth of direction.
Now I am surrounded by children

in a beautiful old house.
Every night we cry ourselves to sleep.

4

Back on my old ship   bound for war.

Red rock & sand
dark purple skies.
                Always watched   always lost.

Skeletal ships   partially flooded.

A goat floats by
                                bloated
in a rainbow sheen of oil.

*

One-hundred degree fog —
escape into the ship,
into my berth,
into a book.

I write my way toward escape.
I am a slow moving target.

5

          Navigating clear
                    of poison clouds.
No one   is concerned
          gas masks are cracked.

My brother   speaks with whales
          on the starboard side.

The real gas masks are lost
bobbing in our wake.

*

I only tell translatable stories.

The morning a humpback drifted alongside —
wild & immense:
they could imagine how that felt.

But the immense futility of warfare
training: untranslatable.

6

Ship sinking.
Lost deep below decks
in spaces with no light.
A hatch opens

to a passageway of locked hatches,

Calm sinks in
as I give up
under purple water.

*

new sailors were blindfolded,
had to escape from their berthing.
How funny it was to watch them
bang around until they gave up.

Lesson: there is no escape,
don't get trapped.

7

Back aboard my last ship

my last ship is sinking again.

No one understands.

Not my ship anymore:
now it's my Grandfather's: *USS Boxer.*

He doesn't know me,
doesn't have time to explain the navy way.

White planes circle overhead.

*

In my dreams, the dead are ashamed.
Their loss is a fault to be ignored,
though obvious, like a missing finger or eye.
When I ask what death will be,

they grow impatient,
leave me in the calm before waking.

8

Heavy seas roll
like distant hills.

The ship was all rise

& fall.

Foam streaks   drew lifelines

across my palms.

Lifelines   along   the weather deck

slack into her last summer.

*

When I woke to alarms,
I thought I was still dreaming.
The ship's belly had been sliced
& was bleeding black oil

lines woven through our wake.
A new port waits to heal us.

Psalm for Hemlock Cove

Low tide reveals wetland mussels.

Wind ripples Hemlock Cove.

The red horizon is certain of Fall
while gulls circle above our boat.

Today, my son is content to toss a line
& draw it back into the boat.

Snapper & blue-claw crabs
dart from his baitless threat.

Marsh crickets know summer fades
but we refuse to believe
anything we love will end.

anchor pulled —
snowy egret watches

summer leaves

Notes

Seascapes

In 1806, Commander Francis Beaufort of the British Navy first noted his scale for estimating the force of wind based on its visible effects on the sea. Beaufort's Wind Force Scale is still used by mariners today as a means to predict the weather and prepare for its effects. Italicized phrases in the poem are Beaufort's own words. The wind poems (centered), also draw language and inspiration from the Beaufort Wind Scale.

Man Overboard

A "seahawk" is a military helicopter (Sikorsky SH-60). The "brig" is a military prison, especially in the navy.

Mass Casualty Drill

A Mass Casualty Drill is an exercise that simulates a multiple casualty situation onboard a US Navy ship, generally in conjunction with another battle readiness exercise.

Drownproof

This sequence draws upon various sources of US Navy guides for survival, primarily the 1964 Special Issue: "Safety and Survival At Sea," *All Hands Magazine*.

The Watch Officer's Guide to TAO

The sequence is a found poem with text drawn from *Watch Officer's Guide*, eleventh edition, Naval Institute Press, 1979. The italicized, right aligned portions are selections from the *Tao te Ching*, translation by Stephen Mitchell. In the U.S. Navy, the Tactical Action Officer (TAO) is in tactical control of the ship, especially in regards to threat-analysis and reaction. TAO also refers to the essential principle / way of Taoism.

Forenoon Watch

A Machinist's Mate is an enlisted person responsible for the maintenance and operation of a ship's propulsion systems and machinery. The "Main Space" is one of the ship's main propulsion spaces.

Chief Fisher's Song

A Chief Petty Officer in the US Navy is a senior non-commissioned officer.

Walk on Water

This is a found poem. All text was erased from the lectionary of the mass for Tuesday of the 18th Week in Ordinary Time.

Acknowledgements

My deep gratitude to the editors of the following journals, in which some of these poems first appeared:

"Son of Waves" (part 4 of "Water-born") — *Prairie Schooner*

"Drownproof," "First Night at War," and "Forenoon Watch" — *Action, Spectacle*

"Dhow Close Astern" — *O-Dark-Thirty*

"Sea Heaps Up" — *Drunken Boat*

"Mass Casualty Drill" — *Unbroken Journal*

"Celestial Navigation" — *The Harpoon Review*

"Near Gale" — *Manhattanville Review*

"Lost at Sea" — *War Literature & the Arts: An International Journal of the Humanities*

"Scattered White Horses" — *CURA: A Literary Magazine of Art and Action*

I would also like to thank Brian Clint for his willingness to help bring these poems to the world.

Peter Vanderberg is the founding editor of Ghostbird Press. He served in the US Navy from 1999 – 2003 and received an MFA in Poetry from CUNY Queens College. His work has appeared in journals such as *Prairie Schooner*, *Drunken Boat*, *Modern Haiku*, and *CURA*, and his chapbook *Crossing Pleasant Lake* is available from Red Bird Press. He lives on Long Island with his wife and four children.